CONTENTS

on or before the last date shown below.

Are you listening?

Other titles of interest

Age and change: Models of involvement for older people
Tony Carter and Peter Beresford

Exploring unmet need: The challenge of a user-centred response
Mary Godfrey and Gill Callaghan

Unmet need and older people: Towards a synthesis of user and provider views
Lis Cordingley, Jane Hughes and David Challis

Older people's definitions of quality services
Hazel Qureshi and Melanie Henwood

Are you listening?

*Current practice in information, advice and
advocacy services for older people*

Pat Margiotta, Norma Raynes, Dimitri Pagidas,
John Lawson and Bogusia Temple

JR
JOSEPH
ROWNTREE
FOUNDATION

The **Joseph Rowntree Foundation** has supported this project as part of its programme of research and innovative development projects, which it hopes will be of value to policy makers, practitioners and service users. The facts presented and views expressed in this report are, however, those of the authors and not necessarily those of the Foundation.

Joseph Rowntree Foundation
The Homestead
40 Water End
York YO30 6WP
Website: www.jrf.org.uk

ISBN 1 85935 105 0   (paperback)
ISBN 1 85935 106 9   (pdf: available at www.jrf.org.uk)

A CIP catalogue record for this report is available from the British Library.

Cover design by Adkins Design

Prepared and printed by:
York Publishing Services Ltd
64 Hallfield Road
Layerthorpe
York
YO31 7ZQ
Tel: 01904 430033   Fax: 01904 430868   Website: www.yps-publishing.co.uk

Further copies of this report, or any other JRF publication, can be obtained either from the JRF website (www.jrf.org.uk/bookshop/) or from our distributor, York Publishing Services Ltd, at the above address.

ACKNOWLEDGEMENTS

To produce this report we had the help of a number of people. Our local steering group members helped with their advice and comments and provided contacts for us in local communities. As a result of their guidance we were able to meet people who helped us contact older people who gave us the benefit of their views and experience in getting information, advice and advocacy. We are grateful to all of them for the time they gave us and their encouragement and interest in the project.

Our steering group members were Mrs Barbara Bleeker, Mr H. Bobat, Ms Elaine Clark, Ms Claudette Webster and Dr M. Vernon.

Helping us meet older people in different locations were Sister T. Hughes, Ms Maureen Davidson and Ms Pat Warburton.

In our university we were helped by the library staff and in particular Julie Hesmondhalgh who were extremely helpful in aiding our literature search.

Special thanks are also due to the support staff in the Institute of Health and Social Care Research at the University of Salford. Mrs Elaine Smith, Ms Katherine Tress and Ms Anna Bancsi helped us prepare the drafts and the final report.

1 INTRODUCTION AND RECOMMENDATIONS

Introduction

The importance of providing clear relevant information, advice and advocacy for older people is increasingly being recognised by health care professionals, politicians and policy makers. Dunning (1999) reports that an Inter-Ministerial Group on ageing had been established with three key themes of

- productive ageing

- health and social care

- consultation and involvement of older people.

Within this context a number of significant attempts to promote the well-being of older people and involve them in development and implementation have occurred. One of these has been Better Government for Older People (BGOP) which was launched in 1998 as a two-year action research programme. The aim of this programme is to improve services for older people by better meeting their needs, listening to their views, providing clearer and more accessible information and encouraging and recognising their contribution. The 28 BGOP pilot sites across the UK developed partnerships with public, private and voluntary agencies and older people to set local objectives and priorities for action. An evaluation of this programme has shown the progress made by local partnerships in pursuing a strategic approach to an ageing population and suggests ways of using the findings to influence policy (Hayden and Boaz, 2000).

A second commitment to older people has been within Better Care, Higher Standards. The Secretary of State announced this charter for long-term care in December 1999, setting out the values on which people can expect their local housing, health and social services to be based. One of the stated values is 'help users to have a voice through advocacy and other representative organizations' which applies to all vulnerable people (Better Care, Higher Standards, 2000). There is a strong message in this charter that good information and communication are seen as the key to providing good, effective services.

A third significant government document is the National Service Framework for Older People (NSF), published in 2001. This framework is stated to be 'the key vehicle for ensuring that the needs of older people are at the heart of the reform programme for Health and Social Services' (Department of Health, 2001, p. 5). The NSF and Better Care, Higher Standards are connected by sharing objectives, working on establishing standards and improving information about the services available to older people.

The establishment in 2002 of the Patient Advice and Liaison Services (PALS) is a further development in the move towards improving services in hospitals for all age groups. Provision of information about health services and the complaints procedure, the resolution of problems where possible and referrals to specialist, independent advocacy services where appropriate are the principal aspects of the service (Department of Health, 2002).

Advocacy for older people has been promoted by the Scottish Executive which, following on from an advocacy conference in 2000, has published two guides on advocacy. The first was a

2

guide to good practice and the second is a guide for health boards, NHS trusts, local authorities and anyone else involved with advocacy. The publication of these guides reflects the importance that Scottish ministers attach to the provision of independent advocacy to enable vulnerable people to have access to representation of their needs, views and wishes (Scottish Executive, 2001).

This is clearly a current and important area of investigation, and of real importance to older people. This report presents the findings from a critical review of current practice in information, advice and advocacy services for older people derived from a literature and web search and focus groups. We give examples of good practice and recommendations for future action.

In Chapter 2 the definitions and interpretations of the terms 'information', 'advice' and 'advocacy' are discussed and a consensus reached about the commonly held views of the terms. Chapter 3 reviews current practice in the provision of information and advice, and Chapter 4 current practice in advocacy services. In Chapter 5 we identify examples of good practice and current guidelines for good practice in the provision of information, advice and advocacy. Chapter 6 reports the findings from the focus groups and compares those findings with the evidence found in the literature.

Recommendations

For information, advice and advocacy there are three overarching principles of good practice. We identified these as follows:

1   The involvement of older people in what we call the DIM process (design, implementation and monitoring of schemes and projects).

2   The centrality of the older person in all provision of
    information, advice and advocacy schemes.

3   The importance of face-to-face communication.

Information and advice

We recommend the following:

- Information via audiotapes should be developed for those
  people who are visually impaired and for those who lack
  literacy skills. We need to be aware that the production of
  leaflets in languages other than English may be cosmetic.
  These leaflets may be produced in the belief that we are
  being culturally sensitive but for the older people who
  cannot read they are useless.

- There is a need to improve access to computers for older
  people on a local basis, perhaps by the development of
  cyber cafés in community centres.

- Further research should be carried out into the efficacy of
  information provision, especially in regard to minority ethnic
  groups.

- There needs to be wider, more appropriate distribution of
  written information in places where older people live their
  lives day to day.

- Information on the websites and in all other forms of
  provision must be updated regularly.

Advocacy

We recommend the following:

- Older people should be provided with information about local advocacy services – their availability and ease of access.

- The older vulnerable person must be central in the advocacy process.

- Advocacy must be individually led by the person in need.

- Older people should be involved at all levels, whether in planning, organising or acting as volunteer advocates.

- Volunteer citizen advocates should be drawn from the many diverse groups and cultures within a community.

- Health and social care practitioners should receive training about advocacy and the role of volunteer advocates.

- Funding should be made available to support advocacy schemes to maintain their independence.

- National standards and codes of practice should be established. These would include guidelines for recruitment, training and supervision of volunteers.

2 DEFINITIONS, TERMINOLOGY AND METHODS

Definitions

At the outset of the project it was considered to be important that the terms 'information', 'advice' and 'advocacy' had clear definitions. Initially the following were adopted as 'working' definitions for the purpose of the literature review.

- Information: information giving is the passing on of facts thought to be relevant to a person's situation.

- Advice: advice giving involves making statements that indicate what you think someone should do in a situation.

- Advocacy: advocacy is about speaking up for oneself or on behalf of someone else according to their needs and wishes. (Morgan, undated)

Whilst the above provide a basis for categorising literature and services some further discussion is necessary to illustrate how the three terms are used. The differences can be as subtle as defining advice and information in terms of 'giving', as above, or merely as a 'provision', the latter denoting neutrality or passivity. This could lead to an implication that if information is given, then some element of selection has been taken by the 'giver' on which information to give. The result of such differences is that care needed to be exercised when analysing information on services and the literature. The following brief consideration of some examples of terminology in use will serve to illustrate differences in usage.

Advice and information differ from advocacy inasmuch as they are rarely defined. Groups or organisations offering advocacy tend to provide a definition in their publicity material. From this it can be inferred that there is an assumption that the meaning of advice and information is commonly understood whilst advocacy needs to be explained. Initially, therefore, advice and information will be considered together, with advocacy being taken alone.

Advice and information

A key difference between advice and information is in both the content of the material and the context within which it is given. For example Age Concern Wolverhampton offers 'free advice on community safety and crime reduction matters' (www.wolverhampton.gov.uk). Similarly Help the Aged and British Gas offer 'A free welfare rights advice line, helping callers to take appropriate action about their care and housing issues … and advise them how to make such claims' (www.helptheaged.org.uk). These two examples illustrate that advice usually relates specifically to particular issues, such as grants and welfare rights, which, whilst open to interpretation, have distinct objectives and accessibility criteria. Consequently, once background information on an individual's circumstances has been obtained they can be advised on what course of action to take and how to proceed with it.

Information differs from advice inasmuch as the same material might be made available but it is the individual's role to interpret it and decide on how they might proceed. The provision of information falls broadly into two categories. First, there is material which is freely accessible in various formats. This can be in the form of leaflets, information sheets, websites etc. The second category comprises material which is circulated either generally, e.g. via a mail drop, or to mailing lists. An example of the latter is North Tyneside Pensioners Association which refers to information as being 'disseminated regularly in a large font and is colour coded to avoid confusion' (www.geordie-greypower.org.uk). So, whilst the terms 'advice' and 'information' are used interchangeably they are distinct and need to be seen as having different meanings and applications.

Advocacy

Whilst a straightforward understanding of advocacy might be seen as unproblematic, a consideration of literature provided by organisations offering advocacy indicates that this is not the situation. Indeed, Box (2001, p. 6) found that 'the term "advocacy" has limited currency amongst people who used the Knowsley Advocacy & Information Service'.

As mentioned above promotional literature frequently defines advocacy and the role of 'the advocate'. Citizens Advice Lincolnshire defines advocacy as 'verbal support or argument for a cause or policy'. This somewhat stark definition does not identify advocacy as meeting the needs of individuals. However, a leaflet produced by the organisation referring to 'Help for Older People' states that 'Some older people may need support in making informed choices'. This implies more of an affinity with information and advice than with advocacy. The Knowsley Pensioners Advocacy and Information Service provides a complex definition housed in a list of terms such as 'Advancement ... Backing ... Championing for Defence ... Upholding'. These are being given in response to the question 'What does it all mean?' However, the group's mission statement offers a more succinct definition when it states, 'We provide support to enable our peers to obtain their rights as citizens, so enhancing their quality of life', thereby clearly defining advocacy as a service for individuals (Box, 2001).

Although there is evidence of some lack of clarity in the use of terms and, indeed, the nature of services operating under those terms, a general consensus emerged that:

1   Information is the open and accessible supply of material deemed to be of interest to a particular population. This can be either passively available or actively distributed.

2   Advice offers guidance and direction on a particular course of action which needs to be undertaken in order to realise a need, access a service or realise individual entitlements.

3   Advocacy is the provision of support and encouragement, or representation of individuals' views, needs or rights. It is fundamental that advocacy recognises the centrality of the service user.

Methods

A steering group was established in order to gain access to local services and people who use these services and to advise and comment on the progress of the review. A literature search was carried out using electronic databases and the search terms used were (i) older people and advocacy and (ii) older people and information and advice. A sample of local authority websites was examined to ascertain what information or advice was provided for older people.

Following advice from the information specialists in the Institute of Health and Social Care Research the following databases were searched:

- Caredata
- HMIC
- SSCI
- Assia
- Cinahl
- Medline
- Sociological Abstracts.

The search was limited to UK abstracts from 1990 to 2002. Abstracts were selected that:

- described information, advice and advocacy projects in current practice

- evaluated information, advice and advocacy projects and their guidelines

- discussed terminology.

Abstracts were not selected if they only discussed the importance of information and advice provision or advocacy services for older people but provided no guidelines as to content. In addition to books and professional and academic journals, government websites were searched for significant documents relating to services for older people. Organisations that provide information, advice and advocacy services were contacted for information about current practice.

A systematic review was carried out using a keywording process similar to that used by the Evidence for Policy and Practice Information and Co-ordinating Centre (EPPI-Centre, 2002). A working paper was created for each piece of literature. This process enabled us to identify and exclude literature that did not meet our search criteria. Two independent readers carried out a review of a sample of included and excluded literature with a high level of reliability being agreed.

Three focus groups of older people were convened in order to gain direct information about their opinions and experiences of information and advice giving and advocacy. We also sought their views about what should be included in guidelines for good practice.

A survey of local authorities' websites was carried out. Some of the limitations in Internet research are the sampling technique and the accuracy or reliability of the information. In some cases the websites are providing out-of-date information. With this in mind, we selected a representative sample of the total number of local authorities in the UK. These were stratified according to their type (city, borough, district, county, metropolitan and others) as shown in Figure 1.

Ten per cent of each type were randomly selected. This generated a sample size of 57 local authorities. The search directories used to access these were Lycos and Google.

Figure 1

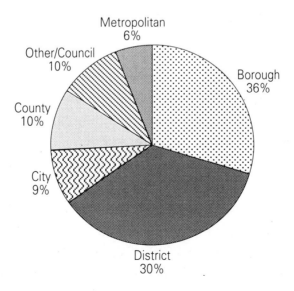

3 WHAT IS CURRENT PRACTICE?

Information and advice

The review of the literature on information and advice, terms which are linked together in the majority of projects and services, shows that there are many different approaches to providing individuals with relevant information and advice within the UK.

Some approaches are general, encompassing a wide range of topics which are relevant to people's lives whatever their age, some are geared more to older people and others address the needs of groups with a specific condition.

A great deal of information is aimed at carers and families of older, vulnerable people. Whilst the focus of this review is the provision of information and advice directly to older people, we found that some of the initiatives described are designed to include all these groups, as well as older people themselves.

From the literature it would appear that information and advice for older people may be provided directly to them or by professionals working in health and social care or the voluntary organisations. The provision of information and advice, whether through direct access or through professionals, in many cases appears to be governed by the views of the provider group or organisation. May (1998) examined whether the information needs of older people in relation to community care had been addressed by the information strategy in one shire county in response to the NHS and Community Care Act 1990. May found evidence that the professionals restricted the amount and type of information that they gave and were known to have withheld information from clients. The majority of the older people involved in the study indicated that they had not been supplied with comprehensive information. One person commented that 'Nobody seems to volunteer up-to-date information and help'. Ownership of information by professionals is not uncommon.

There are examples of information packs being developed for use by professionals rather than for direct access by older people. An inner London project by the Centre for Policy on Ageing designed such a pack, known as the 'orange book', to improve information about local services for older people. In an account of this development Tester (1992) reports that a glance at the membership of the steering group reveals that, apart from a representative from Islington Pensioners Link, no older people in the community were involved. The book is intended for professionals in contact with older people. It would appear that only the older people who are in receipt of services involving face-to-face contact can obtain the information relevant to their needs. Asking older people about their information needs generates the answer that their needs (particularly regarding health) are much the same as those of the wider population (Cawthra, 1999). However, older people with some physical or learning disability or with mental health problems may need information specifically relevant to their individual needs in addition to general information on a wide range of subjects. Research shows that older people in regular contact with health and social care staff because of their specific needs were no more likely to get information than were older people without such contact (May, 1998).

Hinkley and Steele (1992) produced a directory of organisations and groups which provide nationally relevant disability information, recognising that many of the people using their information services will be older people. Age Concern, Help the Aged and

Mind are among the most well-known organisations that provide information and advice generally and specifically. Others, such as RNIB (Royal National Institute for the Blind) and RNID (Royal National Institute for the Deaf), are more focused on providing information and advice regarding the specific impairments of sight and hearing.

Help the Aged provides a national free phone information service for older people that gives advice on topics such as benefits, housing and health. Seniorline, as the service is called, also helps people to gain access to Age Concern groups, social services departments, advice centres and groups providing practical help. Age Concern, as a national organisation, provides information fact sheets. At its local level of independent groups working within local communities it provides information and advice in the local centres and fact sheets are also available on the Age Concern website.

Many of the local Age Concern groups have set up information and advice schemes for older people with specific needs. One example is Age Concern Suffolk. They established ACCESS (the Age Concern Elderly Support Service) in Ipswich in 1986 and a second one in Halesworth in 1992. ACCESS offers a comprehensive 'one stop' confidential service offering people with dementia and their carers information and advice and actively promoting a choice of lifestyle (McManus, 1999). Among the aims of the service is the provision of high quality information on the nature of dementia and advice on coping with symptoms and behaviour. Information is provided about help available from the statutory and voluntary agencies and the service aims to act as advocates on behalf of people with dementia.

Consideration of the needs of specific groups of older people led to Mind developing their information and advice provision to meet their needs. Diverse Minds, Mind's Black and Minority

Ethnic Unit, is working to ensure that all their information and services are culturally sensitive and appropriate to the needs of people in black and minority ethnic communities with mental health problems. There is also the Mindinfoline, a telephone information service offering translation and interpretation of services in over 100 languages.

In the Better Government for Older People (BGOP) project many different initiatives were developed suited to the local communities involved. Some of them developed innovative, inter-agency activities designed to improve older people's access to information and then on to services, benefits, advice about other entitlements and opportunities. In Kensington and Chelsea two reading groups of older people, from local voluntary organisations, were formed to review and revise the council's information about health and care and information across all council departments. Major changes resulted in the way that leaflets are presented, making them easy to read, with improved print size and free of jargon. A leaflet entitled 'Moving in Care', which had passed unremarked by officials, attracted 200 comments from the group (Ellis, 1999).

The Benefits Agency has worked with eight of the pilot projects on improving information provision, aiming to increase benefit take-up by older people. This has resulted in increased enquiries for information and advice and an increase in successful claims for benefits. In Scotland, Stirling Council and the Benefits Agency ran benefits advice roadshows in towns and villages across a wide rural area with great success in helping older people with their claims (BGOP, 2000). The Citizens Advice Bureau (CAB) in Trafford is running a scheme to improve older people's uptake of benefits.

Methods of providing information and advice

Described in the literature are six different methods for the provision of information and advice (Cawthra, 1999):

- written
- verbal
- combined formats such as visual and written and interactive packages
- one-stop shop
- libraries
- websites.

Written

There are often problems in leaflets with jargon, poor layout or font size. The RNIB states that 126,000 65–74 year olds in the UK are blind or partially sighted and that 70 per cent of people with impaired vision are over 75 years. They experience an increased need for relevant information together with a decline in ability to obtain the information in written format. Many older visually impaired people use large print and/or audiotapes as their main source of information rather than Braille. Those who used Braille in the past may have lost the ability because of ageing. The RNIB provides valuable help for those designing websites in order to ensure maximum accessibility (Blake, 1998).

Dunning (1998a) states that older people in minority ethnic groups with mental health problems have difficulty in accessing written information. A community health project worker commented that 'Leaflets don't help. Some older people don't have literacy skills in their own language. They also don't know the jargon used within the information available. It is meaningless'.

- Barnsley District General Hospital with European Union funding set up a web-based information service on health and social services for local older people which includes designing appropriate user interfaces (e.g. touch screen) and training older people in browsing techniques. The web can be a valuable resource to people with visual impairment (Cawthra, 1999).

- Magazines and newspapers are a source of some types of information and advice, either through question and answer columns or listing local services, activities and events. May (1998), in her research carried out with older people, found evidence that local newspapers may be effective methods of providing information to older people.

- Poster display boards in surgeries, health centres, libraries, information and community centres are common sources of information for all age groups. No evidence was found regarding the usefulness of these displays (May, 1998).

Verbal

- There are many helplines in action, free phone health information services and NHS Direct plus those run by charities such as Age Concern, and the Help the Aged telephone service Seniorline.

- Care Direct is the most recent government initiative for the provision of information and advice. This will be a 'one-stop gateway' with the main phone number open 24 hours a day and local help desks with longer daytime availability. The service will provide consistent comprehensive information about social care, social security, health and housing. Six local authorities in the South West are piloting this scheme and the plan is to cover the whole of the South West from October 2002 and to extend it across England over the next four years (Valios, 2001). The project manager for Devon social services states that 'the establishment of Care Direct is an exciting opportunity to improve and enhance significantly the way in which information, advice and help are made available to older people and their carers' (Searle, 2001, p. 37).

- Professionals and voluntary workers provide verbal information and advice in various settings where older people meet or attend for help.

Combined formats

There are a number of examples of combined formats in delivering information and advice:

- A service set up in one health authority has text telephones in surgeries and health centres for use by people who are deaf or hearing impaired. This is supported by written information in the form of leaflets.

- Information may be presented on video in surgeries and health centres perhaps on a continuous loop. There is often supporting written information in the form of a poster display and leaflets.

- There are interactive packages which can bring together different sources of information and help with interpretation of the information. An example of this is the touch screen project IRIS at Camden and Islington Primary Care Trusts.

- The King's Fund's Promoting Patient Choice project has worked with other trusts to set up multimedia packages of information and advice. (Cawthra, 1999)

One-stop shop

- Under One Roof was set up in 1998 and is managed by Lewisham and Guys Mental Health NHS Trust. This brought together professionals, benefits staff and voluntary workers all in one place. It was aimed at single homeless people, many in the older age groups, giving immediate access to information and a wide range of services.

Libraries

- Westminster Public Libraries set up the Weldis programme that offers older and disabled people access electronically, not just in libraries but also in health centres and social services information points, to information on health issues and services, housing and benefits.

- There is a Healthpoint information service situated in Poole Central Library.

- A similar service is provided by the Katz Health Information and Resource Centre at Poole Hospital and the information service at the Luster Hospital, Stevenage. (Cawthra, 1999)

Websites

Perhaps the main growth area for some organisations providing information and advice is in the use of websites. The belief that older people do not use computers is said to be a myth and the number of older people having access to and using the Internet is increasing annually (Cawthra, 1999). National opinion poll statistics in 1997 recorded that 6 per cent of Internet users in the UK were over 55 years of age. The main UK sites for older people are those of Age Concern, the Centre for Policy on Ageing and Help the Aged.

- Age Concern's site carries news about government's policies regarding older people. It also publishes its fact sheets on the web.

- The Centre for Policy on Ageing aims to stimulate awareness of the needs of older people and to promote debate about issues affecting older age groups.

- The Help the Aged website provides a comprehensive list of subjects that can be accessed for information and a list of the services it provides. (Blake, 1998)

Local authority websites as a source of information and advice for older people

The results of our exploration of the availability and ease of access to information and advice for older people in a sample of 57 local authority websites are presented below.

We interrogated each website with a pro forma using the following questions:

- Can I access local authority websites using common search engines?

- Is there a button or arrow directly to advice and information for older people?

- Is there a social/community services page?

- How many steps are there to reach advice and information?

- Does the page provide information specific to older people?

- Was the information available in languages other than English?

- Was the page kite-marked for visually impaired people?

Accessibility
- To be of benefit a local authority website should be easily accessible. In our sample, the majority (96.5 per cent) of the sites could be accessed by common search engines such as Google and Lycos.

- After accessing the site the easiest way for the authorities to provide services for older people is to have a direct link (button) on the first page that will guide older people to the information. Despite this only two (3.5 per cent) of the sample of 57 local authorities had a direct link to issues for older people.

- In the absence of a direct link one alternative is to look for a social/community services page. Thirty-one (54.5 per cent) of the authorities provided the visitors to their site with a link to such a page.

- We found that it was not always easy to access the social services pages. Of the visited sites 48.5 per cent needed two or three steps (clicks) in order to reach the proper page. It is important to note that in almost one-third of the sites (32.2 per cent), in order to access the social services page, more than four clicks were needed. This makes it obvious that accessing the information is not easy.

- Accessing the social services page does not necessarily mean access to information for older people. The research shows that 32 (56.1 per cent) of the visited local authority websites were not providing any information especially for older people within any page of their website. There were 25 (43.9 per cent) who did provide such information.

- The availability of the information in languages other than English is important. Only 14 per cent of the sample authorities provided such a service. (For good practice examples see http://www.chesterfieldbc.gov.uk, http://www.iwight.gov.uk/ and http://www.wearvalley.gov.uk.)

- We explored the accessibility of the sites for visually impaired people. Of the examined sites 93 per cent lacked kite-marked pages. Of the remaining four (7 per cent) only two (3.5 per cent) of the sites were marked on the first page.

The content of the local authority websites is typically made up of general information about the local authority and specific information about services. We have tried to represent the average distribution of contents in Figure 2. Analysis of all 57 websites showed that the majority (78.94 per cent) of the local authorities are providing general information. In addition to this 57.9 per cent are providing information about housing and 49.1 per cent are providing information about leisure. Only a small number, one in ten or less, of the local authorities provided information about health care, transport, falls and finance.

Figure 2 Content of local authority websites

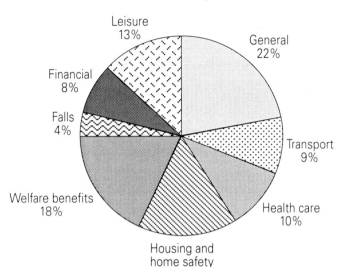

Leisure
13%

General
22%

Financial
8%

Falls
4%

Transport
9%

Welfare benefits
18%

Health care
10%

Housing and
home safety
16%

4 ADVOCACY

Advocacy takes different forms, being promoted and delivered as self-advocacy, peer advocacy, collective advocacy, paid advocacy, legal advocacy and citizen advocacy. The different types have been described by researchers.

Self-advocacy is speaking up for oneself whenever possible. People with learning difficulties have been enabled through the development of self-advocacy to speak out and have their voice heard. Mental health survivors have used self-advocacy to influence policy and practice (Ivers, 1994; Brandon *et al.*, 1995; Atkinson, 1999).

Peer advocacy involves partnership between two people who have experienced disability or mental health problems. Thus, the advocate can draw on that personal 'insider' experience to show understanding and empathy and may be acceptable where other people are not (Brandon *et al.*, 1995; Atkinson, 1999).

Collective advocacy may be referred to as group advocacy or class advocacy. Organisations at national or local level may campaign or speak up for groups of people in order to influence policy and practice. Examples of such organisations are Mind and Age Concern England (Ivers, 1994; Brandon *et al.*, 1995; Atkinson, 1999).

Paid advocacy involves the use of paid advocates who offer advice and support to anybody who seeks their help. This role is provided, for example, by some CAB workers. Some services employ people whose role is to help service users gain whatever they are entitled to receive, for example welfare rights workers (Simons, 1993).

Legal advocacy operates within the law of the country. The advocate, usually a lawyer, will represent the client's interests, speaking on their behalf about a specific problem. The relationship is purely professional (Ivers, 1994).

Citizen advocacy is sometimes called lay advocacy or volunteer advocacy. This form of advocacy consists of a one-to-one relationship between the volunteer and their disadvantaged or vulnerable partner and is independent of any service provider. The advocate represents the interests of their partner as if they were their own. The relationship involves a period of befriending, building up trust and understanding of the person's needs and views so that they are represented as well as possible (Wertheimer, 1993; Ivers, 1994).

It is citizen advocacy that appears to be the type that has grown and developed steadily since the 1980s. In 1998 the Centre for Policy on Ageing identified 60 schemes for older people. Citizen Advocacy, Information and Training (CAIT), at the present time, has 600 schemes across the UK on their database. Valios states there are now up to 800 schemes in the UK catering for the various groups of vulnerable people but does not specify how many are for older people (Valios, 2002).

Some advocacy schemes are generic and relate to people living within certain areas, others are specific to older people or people with mental health problems or learning difficulties (Williams, 1999). Thornton and Tozer (1994) report that the most usual type of advocacy for older people appears to be citizen advocacy. The other forms described in the literature are used by learning difficulties groups and mental health groups. Goldsmith (1996) states that there is insufficient material describing advocacy in action with people with dementia.

Citizen advocacy uses trained volunteer advocates who engage in a one-to-one partnership with a vulnerable person who is unable to exercise their rights and so needs someone to speak for them. This is an ongoing partnership which, according to Card (1990) and Wertheimer (1993), needs to begin with the advocate in a befriending role, building a relationship, developing trust and gaining understanding of the older vulnerable person's views and needs.

Wertheimer (1993) states that individual one-to-one support offered by citizen advocacy is an important part of the language of health and social care. She predicts that the package of care enabling older people to live independently would increasingly consist of services from statutory, voluntary and private sectors. However, the National Service Framework for older people (Department of Health, 2001) makes no mention of people's need for advocacy.

One of citizen advocacy's strengths is the ability to independently represent the interests of individuals. Professionals acting as advocates will often experience the dilemma of weighing up a person's need against the needs of others within the context of finite resources. Tension can exist between the responsibility to a client/patient and the demands of the employers. Social workers, nurses and other professionals support their clients/patients as part of their professional code of practice which states that their first consideration must be the interests and safety of patients and clients. However they are not and cannot be independent. It is argued that independent advocacy is crucial in achieving social justice for those people who have difficulty in making their views known and those who are at risk of exclusion (Scottish Executive, 2001).

Brandon (1998) comments that professionals such as nurses and social workers may compete for and defend their role as advocates and can be resistant to independent advocates. They may undermine advocacy, restrict access to patients/clients and maintain that advocates are only special friends. This finding is supported by Atkinson (1999) in her review of advocacy. In a study carried out in a Scottish health board area, advocacy scheme providers were emphasising the importance of the scheme being as independent as possible in order to avoid conflicts of interest for the staff and managers of the services. In some cases there were deep-seated problems between the staff and advocacy workers. Staff awareness and attitudes were found to be hindering the development of citizen advocacy. A comment made to the interviewer by a member of staff was that 'patients had no rights and that advocacy could be useful in making them [service users] see reason' (Lindsay, 1997).

However, the value of citizen advocacy has been recognised by the professional bodies of the British Medical Association and the Royal College of Nursing. In their joint report on consent and care, while urging caution when involving citizen advocates in confidential discussions, they state that citizen advocates make a valuable contribution in defending vulnerable people's interests: 'It is important that their role is clearly defined and that mutual understanding and co-operation is fostered between advocates, the health care team and the patients involved' (British Medical Association, 1995, p. 38). This issue of independence from providers of care is seen as vital in the advocacy movement (Wertheimer, 1993; Cohen, 1994; Ivers, 1994; Brandon, 1998; Atkinson, 1999; Valios, 2002).

Ivers (1994) writes that Age Concern England suggests that independence is a key feature of advocacy and is necessary if advocates truly aim to represent the interests of their partners and to be loyal to the partnership. Valios (2002) reports that the director of Advocacy Across London warns of the problems if advocacy projects become funded by local and health authorities. They risk losing their independence and conflicts of interests will inevitably arise.

Some advocacy projects involved with older people have had contracts or service-level agreements with the NHS and social services departments. Dunning (1995) finds that this has all too often compromised their independence in that the definition of advocacy has been narrowed to suit the views of the statutory service. A contrary view has been expressed by Bleeker (2002) that funding is necessary and need not compromise the volunteer service. According to CAIT, funding is an ongoing issue for the majority of advocacy groups: 'a lot of groups go for a single source of funding usually from statutory agencies' (Cohen, 1995, p. 54).

Examples of citizen advocacy projects

- Trafford CVS Advocacy Scheme is an independent organisation which receives some funding from the local authority. Independent volunteer advocates represent clients in dealing with their complaints.

- The Alan McLure House Advocacy Project (1999) is an example of providers and volunteer advocates working together successfully. It was set up by the manager of this residential home for older people with dementia together with the Fife Advocacy Project which uses trained volunteer advocates. They spend half a day each week working either one to one or with a small group of residents. The co-ordinator of the Fife Advocacy Project thinks that working in partnership but maintaining independence has benefited everyone involved. Atkinson (1999), in her review, finds that, as the majority of older, vulnerable people are users of the health and social care services, targeted advocacy projects mostly benefit this group.

- The North Staffordshire Advocacy and Older People Project was set up by the Beth Johnson Foundation to provide advocacy for older people who were in receipt of health and social services care. Its aim was to enable older people, including some of the most disabled, to continue living in their own homes. The volunteer advocates are usually older people (Ivers, 1994). Thornton and Tozer (1994) report that many older people involved in community care act as advocates for their more vulnerable contemporaries.

- The Alzheimers Disease Society Advocacy Scheme in Berkshire works to establish partnership with older people who have difficulty in speaking for themselves.

- The Isle of Wight Advocacy Consortium works with people aged over 75. The aim is to represent their interests in their dealings with the support services in their daily lives.

- Citizen Rights for Older People (CROP) is a charity set up by Age Concern Kent and stresses its independence by gaining funding from a variety of statutory and voluntary sources rather than becoming dependent on any one body. The service was developed in response to evidence that there were no advocates for older, frail people who were faced with life-changing decisions.

- Age Concern Coventry provide an advocacy service which is free and independent, aimed at people aged 55 years and over, living within Coventry city boundaries. They provide citizen advocacy, offering an open-ended partnership between volunteer advocate and vulnerable older person, and crisis advocacy which involves solving a one-off problem which may be complex. The client in these cases is able to manage most everyday problems but needs help when some out-of-the-ordinary problem occurs. Williams (1999) reports that a large proportion of referrals require crisis advocacy. Kelly (2000), in the Mind guide to advocacy, says that crisis advocacy is often carried out by paid advocates rather than volunteers.

- Advocacy Partners, one of the projects supported by the Advocacy Council in Surrey, provides crisis and complaints advocacy in addition to citizen advocacy. Complaints advocacy, according to their leaflet, is helping to put things right when they have gone wrong. They say that these advocates are volunteers, independent of services (Atkinson, 1999). The use of volunteer advocates within the minority ethnic communities is growing slowly, building on the awareness of the particular needs of vulnerable minority ethnic older people.

- The Standing Conference of Ethnic Minority Senior Citizens resulted from difficulties experienced by Age Concern London in being able to represent the views and needs of older people from Asian or African-Caribbean backgrounds. One of its aims is to promote the use of advocates when older people visit their GP. Some of the people interviewed stated that their GP was resistant to this (George, 1991).

- Atkinson (1999) gives two examples of schemes, Age Concern Advocacy Project Walsall and Westminster Advocacy Service for Senior Residents, that had successfully recruited Asian and African-Caribbean volunteers as advocates.

- Another example of advocacy services for minority ethnic older people is the African-Caribbean Resource Centre in Nottingham that uses advocacy to promote the interests of African-Caribbean people, especially those who are disadvantaged and suffering from distress.

These advocacy projects in common with the many others operating in the UK use trained volunteers. They recognise that standards are necessary for the protection of clients and advocates and each scheme monitors the service provided. There is, as yet, no national co-ordinating body for the setting of standards in training and practice. However there are several national or regional groups that promote and support the development of advocacy for older people.

CAIT, previously National Citizen Advocacy, fulfils this role on a regional basis for London and the South East. The Highland Community Care Forum in Scotland supports collective self-advocacy projects. Sense Advocacy Development Network promotes, supports and develops advocacy for people with sensory or multiple disabilities. This organisation provides a national service to all groups and individuals committed to advocacy, voluntary or statutory. Advocacy Council in Surrey acts as a training and support agency for citizen advocacy projects in the county. Age Concern England functions nationally as a resource, adviser and campaigner for advocacy for older people and many local Age Concern groups offer an advocacy service.

Wertheimer (1993) called for a national lead body to operate independently of statutory services in a democratic fashion, representing the interests of local advocacy initiatives and promoting and developing citizen advocacy. It could also develop monitoring and evaluation criteria.

The Older People's Advocacy Alliance (OPAAL) UK, on behalf of the Help the Aged Dignity on the Ward campaign, 'calls for a strategic nationwide system, supported by the government with legislation, to provide independent advocacy services for older people in hospital' (OPAAL, 2000).

Echoing the call for a national body the British Medical Association and Royal College of Nursing report (1995) went further in recommending that a registering and disciplinary body be established to monitor and regulate practice in the area of advocacy for older people. According to Valios (2002), training and national standards combine to make the biggest issue in advocacy at present. Valios quotes from Article 6 of the European Convention of Human Rights, which gives everyone the right to a fair hearing, and Article 10, the right to express yourself. How can this have any meaning without advocacy?

According to Atkinson (1999), although advocacy exists in principle for all user groups, it is far from universal in practice and is not there for everyone who needs it.

Access to advocacy is often decided by a combination of factors: historical, geographical and financial. Access starts with the existence of a project in an area but people need to know about it, who and what is it for, how to reach it and what to expect from the service.

5 GOOD PRACTICE AND PRESENT GUIDELINES FOR GOOD PRACTICE

Information and advice

In our review of the literature and websites we have encountered some examples of what is presented as good practice. However, strong evidence of good practice in the provision of information and advice for older people is lacking in much of the literature. Recent government policy documents, as described in Chapter 1, focusing on older people are addressing this issue, aiming to develop good practice and better standards in the provision of care, information and advice.

A recurring theme in the literature is the need to involve older people in the design, implementation and monitoring of information provision. We have called this the DIM process.

The review of the literature also highlights some examples of poor practice. These examples are useful in that they lead to guidelines and suggestions for good practice, as shown in a study carried out by Dunning (1998a) for the Centre for Policy on Ageing, into areas of health and social care that revealed poor provision of information by the statutory services. In particular, the provision of information for older people from black and minority ethnic groups was characterised by inaccuracy, inappropriateness and absence of information that was needed or requested. Having identified the shortcomings, solutions were proposed by black and minority ethnic groups, by older people themselves and by some professionals. These suggestions included the following factors:

- knowing the local population in terms of the diversity of cultures and statistical surveys

- involving older people in the preparation of information provision

- providing information materials in a variety of formats as a matter of course

- disseminating information to where older people live their lives day to day.

One suggestion is that print should be Arial 16 and bold as recommended by the RNIB (Lawson, 2002). This is much clearer and easier for people with visual impairment than just producing larger print. Bleeker (2002) suggests that information, whether written or face to face, could be provided in hairdressers' salons, dentists' surgeries, supermarkets, local post offices, corner shops, leisure centres and bingo halls. Responding to older people's needs in these ways leads to good effective practice because the service is then customer-led. If older people are to be enabled to exercise choice and to make informed decisions about health and social care issues, then their information needs must be met by the service providers' information strategy led by older people themselves.

Three key elements for good practice in an information strategy are suggested in a study carried out by May (1998) exploring the relationship between older people and information. The older people were in receipt of social services care.

The key elements are:

- An understanding that older people comprise a very large group in the general population, not just a group receiving community care services.

- Recognition that current and potential users of care services have a wide, diverse range of information needs.

- An understanding of the information-seeking behaviour of older people, the most acceptable methods of information provision and an awareness of barriers to accessing information.

- Older people should be involved in the monitoring and evaluation of information provision.

- All information materials must be accurate, comprehensive, relevant and up-to-date.

The findings of the study indicated that the use of local broadcasting media and local newspapers may be an effective method of information provision for older people. On a national level some progress has been made towards improving access to appropriate, accurate information. The Better Government for Older People programme has achieved positive results in many of the 28 pilot projects across the UK in addressing older people's expressed views and needs in many aspects of their lives. Older people have been involved in creating change in services that respond more directly to their needs. In Coventry new methods of communicating with more excluded older people are being pioneered, such as letter writing, telephone links and an Internet network.

The evaluation of the pilot schemes by Hayden and Boaz (2000) found that older people wanted co-ordinated 'person-based' information delivered face to face and by telephone. Older people also wanted to actively contribute to producing and delivering information that met their needs.

A comparison of the effectiveness of face-to-face and postal delivery of health and welfare information to older people in south London, carried out by Tester and Meredith (1987), found that face to face was the most effective method of informing and encouraging older people in the use of the services. From this study it was clear that face to face often included an amount of advocacy work. Information with advocacy was more effective than information alone.

The Royal Borough of Kensington and Chelsea scheme involved older people being consulted and expressing their views and need for good quality written information. They also had strong views regarding access to the information. The recommendations were that organisations should work together to rationalise their publications and to maximise distribution. The view was held that information about care services should focus on older people's needs rather than on the services themselves (Ellis, 1999). In order to base information and advice their views and experience must be taken into account rather than being based on what the providers deem to be necessary and/or helpful. This reinforces the user-led/user involvement message.

Basing an outreach service on the expressed needs of older people led to the developments of HOOPS, a new independent local voluntary organisation set up in Birmingham in October 2001. The elected board has representatives from the local community and from statutory and voluntary organisations including Age Concern Birmingham.

The service is the result of a research study commissioned by St Peter's (Saltley) Housing Association. The aim was to discover what kind of services could help older people to maintain independence, promote their health and prevent or delay deterioration of their health. The interviewers for the study were older people themselves. Resulting from the study five preventive services were identified including information, advice and advocacy. The housing association has published an account of the methods and steps taken to develop this service in a good practice guide (Research Update, 2002).

Good practice for older people, included in a study carried out by Hayden *et al.* (2001) and commissioned by the Department of Social Security, means

- information and advice being customer-focused

- appropriate methods of delivery

- the use of formats that are easy to access for older people.

Professionals and older people both have useful knowledge that should be shared and used for the benefit of the services and the service users. There is no evidence to show whether older people were consulted prior to the development of the Help the Aged (2002) information point on their website. This site is easy to access with a clear layout and contains a comprehensive list of issues of interest to older people across the country.

Help the Aged also provide a free telephone helpline called Seniorline that has proved to be very successful. In the year 2000 it received 84,000 enquiries. According to their annual report of 2001 thousands of older people went on to claim benefits they would otherwise have lost. How older people find out about the telephone number is not clear in the literature. The number of people using this service is some measure of proof that older people will discuss their needs over the telephone in contrast to the reported poor use of NHS Direct by people aged over 55, which may be due to a reluctance to access health advice via the telephone (Valios, 2001). Perhaps the reason for this is that most older people will be in contact with or able to contact their GP or practice nurse for help whereas they may be unsure or unwilling to approach the statutory services about their financial situation and so can use Seniorline anonymously if so desired.

The following two examples of schemes which appear as good practice involve older people themselves in the planning and production of information publications. Age Exchange Bedfordshire involved older people in producing a consumer guide to local services and Wigan and Leigh Pensioners Link have elderly people responsible for collating information, writing a dictionary of services and distributing the information (Thornton and Tozer, 1994).

Age Concern England (2000) have published a good practice guide to involving older people and promoting user participation in the development of services. This is based on Age Concern's experience of working with older people.

In contrast to these approaches an information-giving project in an inner London area, focusing on the types of information that older people might need, apparently did not consult any lay older people about their information needs. The information pack was designed to be used by professionals and voluntary workers caring for or visiting older people and not directly by older people (Tester, 1992). The question arises about access to the information for older people not in receipt of health and social services care. Why was the 'orange book', as the pack was called, not made available in places such as libraries and health centres so that the information was accessible to all older people if needed? The project highlighted the facts that information must be clear, accurate, concise and regularly updated.

The provision of accurate, clear, up-to-date information is central to the Care Direct service introduced by the Department of Health in 2001. This service is the result of consultation with older people, carers, their representative organisations and service providers from across the public, voluntary and private sectors. Care Direct, which has been piloted in six local authorities in the South West of England, is expected to function nationally within the next four years and aims to be a model of good practice providing information and advice on a wide range of topics covering health and social care issues, housing and benefits for older people and providing links to other organisations. The service is accessed through NHS Direct. Callers need to make one telephone call only and will receive advice and relevant information on all issues raised plus referrals as appropriate. In addition to the telephone service there is a website for those with access to a computer and drop-in facilities for those who are mobile. Staff in the pilot schemes believe that the service will work and prove to be a model of good practice (Searle, 2001; Valios, 2001).

Summary

We have selected examples of good practice and guidelines for good practice from a variety of initiatives and projects.

The themes emerging from this review about key elements in good practice are:

1   The involvement of older people in finding out what information and advice is needed by older people.

2   The involvement of older people in the design and preparation of the material.

3   The involvement of the older people in the delivery, in some cases, of the information material.

4   The involvement of older people in the monitoring and evaluation of information and advice material that is produced.

5   The efficacy of providing information face to face.

Advocacy

Guidelines for good practice are easier to find in relation to advocacy. Among the many advocacy schemes in existence there are positive, successful examples. There are also examples of schemes where difficulties arise with some professional carers and service providers who resist the involvement of an independent advocate whom they view as encroaching on their area of care. An example of a scheme where difficulties were present but resolved is the Age Concern Tendring Advocacy Scheme. Nurses were suspicious at first when an advocate appeared to support an elderly woman patient in hospital, seeing the volunteer as a 'do-gooder' who would interfere with their work. After a few visits with the volunteer working at easing communication between the patient, the advocate and the nurses and doctors the patient was helped to feel less alone. She was able to express her needs, supported by the advocate, and the staff then accepted the positive contribution of the advocate. The scheme co-ordinator reported that by approaching the work in a sensitive, enquiring manner and building up trust, the benefits for the nurses and the well-being of the ward are apparent to everyone. This is good practice (Cohen, 1995).

Scheme co-ordinators are essential to the functioning of the service. They ensure that volunteers are trained, they usually meet with the older person and then match a volunteer to that person and they will liaise with professional staff who are involved in care, if appropriate. The North Staffordshire Advocacy and Older People Project involves discussion with nurses regarding the boundaries within which they work, the role of the advocate and the benefits to everyone concerned of independent advocacy. Nurses have many patients to care for who may confide in them, thus creating tension for the nurse between expectations of employers and loyalty to patients. The advocate has a one-to-one relationship in which the older person is aware that the advocate is there just for them and their interests (Cohen, 1994).

Acceptance of the principles of citizen advocacy would make it difficult for any professional worker to offer advocacy to a person in their care. The following principles are set down as essential to good practice and are included in a number of codes of good practice developed by organisations involved in the promotion of citizen advocacy (Wertheimer, 1993; Ivers, 1994; Dunning, 1995).

- Independence. There should be no conflict of interests. It is important that the advocate is independent of service providers and of the partner's family and carers.

- One-to-one relationship. A partnership is formed between the older person and the volunteer advocates. This ensures that the advocate focuses on the interests of their partner alone and represents those interests as if they were their own. This is not possible for a professional worker who has the care of many people.

- Allegiance. The advocate must be loyal to the partner alone in order to truly represent that person's interests.

- Unpaid. The citizen advocate is a volunteer who is giving this service because of their desire to help, not because of being paid. This links with being independent of an employer who may have different considerations about the care and future of the older person.

- Long-term. Whenever possible the partnership between the older person and the advocate should be seen as long-term. Time is needed to get to know the partner and to understand their needs and wishes.

- Diversity. Citizen advocacy should recruit and use volunteers from a variety of backgrounds, age and experience. In some schemes many of the volunteers are older people.

The North Manchester Pensioners Association facilitated the active participation of older people in the provision of an advocacy service. Its LINKAGE project includes an advocacy and advice centre staffed by paid workers and older volunteers (Thornton and Tozer, 1994).

Citizen advocacy, in using volunteers from diverse backgrounds in the community, helps to challenge ageist attitudes which can isolate vulnerable older people. The emphasis on equality in the advocate/partner relationship with respect and value accorded the older person is a positive way of redressing the negative view of older people as dependent and disabled (Wertheimer, 1993).

Help the Aged (2001) produced a report which highlighted sections of the Human Rights Act 1998 that are relevant to older people and they encourage older people and their advocates to use the Act to ensure equality and to end discrimination. Practical advice is offered by the organisation on how to use the Act to advantage.

An example of good practice in advocacy is the Alan McLure House Advocacy Project which was the winner of the Best Practice Award in 1999. The manager of this home for older people with dementia, in response to the needs of the residents, set up the scheme together with the Fife Advocacy Project. The trained volunteers spend half a day per week working either one to one or with a small group of older people. The co-ordinator of the Fife project reported that there are great benefits to this joint approach where independent advocates are used within a provider service and everyone works towards agreed outcomes for the benefits of the residents.

In England an example of service providers' commitment to promoting and increasing the availability of independent advocacy is the production of an Advocacy Handbook by Cambridgeshire County Council Social Services Department (2002). The handbook is for service users and for existing and planned advocacy groups. Advocacy and the purpose of advocacy are explained. There is a code of practice and a directory of organisations offering advocacy. The director of the social services department maintains that the key role played by voluntary organisations is recognised and valued and that their aim is to work together.

Co-operation between the voluntary advocacy schemes and the statutory services is growing and will lead to better understanding and improved services for older people. In Enfield the local council for voluntary service together with people from Age Concern and the Alzheimer's Society planned advocate training for social services managers and in Merton similar action was taken. Age Concern in many London boroughs has engaged in co-operative initiatives with social services which include training (O'Neill Crossman, 1994).

The provision of training for advocates is essential to good practice. One of the projects aimed at training volunteers to act as advocates for frail, elderly people who were being assessed for community care packages. The network of advocates was to be built up by the Greater London Forum for the Elderly. In addition to the development of skills the training included the special needs of frail older people and the needs of vulnerable older people in the black and minority ethnic communities (O'Neill Crossman, 1994).

Another organisation active in the London area is Advocacy Across London which is planning to introduce a minimum level of training for advocates. A training group involving key agencies has been set up in an attempt to resolve the inconsistency in standards and training that currently exists (Valios, 2002).

In addition to this development a working group of London advocacy schemes set up by Advocacy Across London has produced an Advocacy Charter. The charter defines a set of core principles for advocacy which, it is hoped, will be adopted by all the London advocacy schemes (Advocacy Across London, 2002).

The aim of achieving good practice in the advocacy service for older people across the UK underpins the calls for a national body to set standards for training and practice and to regulate, monitor and evaluate the service. Such a body could also engage in dialogue with central government regarding issues such as funding strategies and legislation (Wertheimer, 1993). At the present time independent citizen advocacy has no legal status and it depends upon enlightened staff in the statutory and voluntary sectors to promote, nurture and support it and to provide models of good practice (Dunning, 1998b).

Summary

From our selection of examples of good practice we find that emerging from the guidelines are ten themes that should underpin good practice in advocacy services. These are:

1   Building up trust. Effective citizen advocacy depends on the relationship between advocate and partner developing trust and understanding.

2   Advocacy schemes need a scheme co-ordinator who ensures that volunteer advocates are trained, supported and well matched to the vulnerable older people with whom they will be working.

3   Effective communication with health and social care professionals so that the role of the advocate is understood and accepted.

4   Independence of advocate so that there is no conflict of interest.

5   A one-to-one relationship in which the advocate represents their partner alone.

6   Allegiance. Loyalty to the older person by the advocate.

7   The advocate is unpaid. This links with the principle of avoiding conflicts of interest. The advocate has no obligation to an employer.

8   A long-term relationship is seen as advantageous to both older person and advocate so that knowledge and understanding of the older person's needs develop.

9 Citizen advocates should be drawn from the diverse backgrounds, ages and experience within a community.

10 Training is seen as essential to good practice together with the setting of standards and monitoring of the service.

6 OLDER PEOPLE'S VIEWS ON INFORMATION, ADVICE AND ADVOCACY

Older people will have their own views on what constitutes good information, advice and advocacy. These may be reflected in professional perspectives or they may not. To explore the older persons' views we convened three focus groups. The age range of those participating was 66 to 92. The gender balance was nine men and 26 women. The total number of people involved in the groups was 35. A number of the participants had hearing deficits, two were blind and three were in wheelchairs.

Methods

The focus groups took place in three settings. One was a sheltered housing complex attended by tenants and three people who lived in their own homes in the local community and attended social events in the sheltered housing complex. The second was a rehabilitation and assessment ward for day patients in a local hospital and the third was a local healthy hips and hearts group, taking place in a hospital. The participants in this last group were from the community. The participants were citizens in four different local authorities: Salford, Manchester, Stockport and Trafford.

Four questions were put to each of the groups. These were:

1   What kind of advice and information do/would you find it useful to have?

2   What do you consider to be the best way of getting your information and advice?

3   Has anyone used an advocate?

4   If you needed an independent person to speak on your behalf what would be the best way from your point of view to find such a person?

The responses were recorded on a flip chart and then read back to the group to check for accuracy.

Information and advice

The kinds of information and advice that were wanted are listed below.

1   Advice on how to level paths – make flags even, so you don't trip.

2   A list of agencies saying who does what and their phone numbers.

3   How to get trees cut down.

4   How to get information about the future of the residential warden.

5   Getting information to deal with day-to-day worries, e.g. delay in getting boiler replaced.

6 Getting information when you ask for it, not being told they will phone you back or getting music and hanging on.

7 How you can get first-class information in the shortest time, e.g. bath seat.

8 How to get Salford Corporation to do the jobs they are supposed to do, e.g. bin collection – nine months' delay for chief executive reply and still waiting for some action to be taken.

9 Information from Age Concern – things people don't know about, e.g. this clinic.

10 Anything about aids you can use – to help deal with their complaint, e.g. something to use in your home, e.g. help to raise you up in bed.

11 Information about mobility – to help you get about, e.g. taxi vouchers.

12 Information about mobility allowance.

13 Information about carers.

14 To get around and about, to go out to the shops or anything like that, e.g. good neighbours scheme.

15 About days out.

16 Information about a place like Minehead where you can go to do different things each day.

17 Information about what voluntary organisations can do.

18 Information about what social services can do for you.

19 Information about holidays and having a break.

20 Information about CARECALL – the pendant and different ways to pay for it.

21 Help with care.

22 Were they covered by local authority insurance when they used local amenities/services?

23 Who is responsible for repairing burst pipes on property?

24 Advice on information, e.g. phone charges/electricity/gas – having info relieves anxiety.

Best ways of getting advice and information

Face to face

The Citizens Advice Bureau (CAB) was mentioned in each of the groups as a good way of getting information or advice and the importance of face-to-face communication for both of these was underlined in each setting. The CAB provides a good example of this and also now provides domiciliary visits to support its information and advice functions, as the members of the focus groups reported to us. It also provides the under-one-roof information centre that some people saw as useful. The location of such a source in a library or commonly used location was commented upon favourably.

Peers were seen as a source of both advice and information in all three groups.

In the sheltered housing complex the resident warden was seen as a primary source of information and advice. There was concern that the council would remove her as part of a cost-saving exercise.

Media

Whilst some people saw the radio as a good source of information others pointed out that this could be missed, as was the case with television which had the added disadvantage that it was not accessible to people who were blind or had serious visual handicaps. However a local radio station which was dedicated to solving problems and providing information and guidance for older people was highly commended, especially since the presenter did not talk down to older people.

Written

The importance of getting material in writing was identified in two of the groups. The significance of having information in writing in a letter was that it could be referred to in need.

Telephone lines

All the groups saw as important the provision of a list of contact telephone numbers for relevant agencies to be sent out by the council or Age Concern, for example, and for it to be annually updated (or more frequently) to ensure that the information it contained was up-to-date. Out-of-date information was a source of frustration for people. Irritation was expressed about telephone-accessed services which asked people to ring them back. A timely response, that is, immediate or a promise to ring back with information, was what was required.

Websites

There was unanimity that websites were not the best way to find information or advice. Most people did not have access to a computer and many did not want to have such access. Whilst national data suggest rapid growth as characteristic of computer usage amongst older people, it is still the case that the minority of older people possess or have access to computers.

Discussion

Older people's views overlap with the literature in the following ways:

1   The importance and value of face-to-face communication. In the literature the significance of person-to-person contact as a source of information and advice is a key theme of good practice. The views of the older people involved in our focus groups would underline the significance of this characteristic of good practice.

2   Reinforcement of verbal information by written letters or leaflets is emphasised by the groups and in the literature as being more effective than a single method of communication.

3   Telephone access to information and advice mentioned by the groups as causing irritation is also an issue in the literature. Care Direct aims to provide a more responsive service that meets the caller's needs then and there or provide a telephone link to an appropriate agency.

4   The importance of information being accurate and up-to-date was a strongly held view in both the literature and the groups, wherever and however it is provided. Lists of agencies and services with contact names and telephone numbers, mentioned by all the groups as being useful, are contained in some local council free newspapers delivered

to all homes in the borough. Some of these lists do not indicate precisely what services can be accessed by telephone, except in some professionally defined manner, which may have little meaning to a lay person. Councils or some other organisation, perhaps the CAB, could take responsibility for the provision of specific and up-to-date information.

The findings from the focus groups differ from the literature in the following ways:

1   The use of websites to access information did not appeal to the older people in the focus groups. In the literature there were differing views and findings about the increase in computer usage by older people. A point made was that many older people will not be able to afford a computer, attend computer skills courses or have the ability to visit computer centres in places such as libraries.

2   The members of the focus groups made no reference to the involvement of older people in the preparation and dissemination of relevant information and advice. This is an issue that is emphasised in the literature as being important, reported as being part of many local and national initiatives and vocalised by older people involved in some of the studies reviewed.

3   The significance of the resident warden as a source of information and advice for the older people in the sheltered housing complex was highlighted by the older people. In the literature reviewed we found only one mention of this aspect of the warden's role.

4 The older people referred to the CAB as a source of information and advice. Little reference is made to this long-established community-based voluntary organisation in the literature. It is, unlike Age Concern and Help the Aged, not dedicated to older people's issues but clearly has a breadth of knowledge that older people find useful. It provides a service in a person-to-person way including, as we learned, home visits. It is a non-stigmatising source of information and its centrality in these people's lives does seem significant.

Advocacy

No one in any of the groups had used an independent advocate outside a legal context and no one had ever heard of such a service.

Best ways to get advocacy services

In the focus group that took place in the sheltered housing complex older people identified their resident warden as their independent advocate. They mentioned a number of avenues as being useful routes to information about advocacy. One of these referred to in two of the groups was the complete list of services seen as a source of information and advice provided by the local authority or a voluntary organisation dedicated to helping older people like Age Concern or a broader-based one such as the CAB. Leaflets from these organisations were also suggested as a helpful route and a visit to the CAB was suggested. One group suggested that a minister of a church would be useful and that a friend would be one source of information about being an independent advocate. In one group the one-stop shop telephone number the council had put in place to enable all enquiries to be routed from one phone call was commended as a means of getting access to advocacy services if they were perceived as needed.

None of the older people in these groups had anything to say about good practice in advocacy because of their lack of knowledge of such services. What they did say was that they would need more information about advocacy and how to access it.

The significance of the resident warden was again highlighted by the focus groups. Perhaps there is a possibility that the warden's role could be expanded to provide access to more people in the neighbourhood in which advocacy schemes are located.

When we consider the number of advocacy projects that are in existence in the UK as reported in Chapter 4, and the fact that no one in any of the groups had heard of such schemes, we must conclude that there is a need for better promotion of and publicity for such services. Older people should have easy access to such help when they are having difficulty in making their needs and views known.

REFERENCES

Advocacy Across London (2002) *Advocacy Charter.* London: Advocacy Across London

Age Concern England (2000) *Involving Older People. Good Practice Guide.* London: Age Concern England

Alan McLure Advocacy Project (1999) 'Making people matter', *Community Care*, 18–24 November, p. v

Atkinson, D. (1999) *Advocacy – a Review.* Brighton: Pavilion Publishing/Joseph Rowntree Foundation

Better Care, Higher Standards (2000) *A Charter for Long Term Care.* www.doh.gov.uk/longtermcare/housing.htm

Better Government for Older People (BGOP) (2000) www.bgop.org.uk/reference/pub160.htm (accessed 28 May 2002)

Blake, M. (1998) Internet Resources for Older People. http://www.ariadne.ac.uk/issue14/older-people/

Bleeker, B. (2002) Personal communication. Chief Officer, Trafford Council for Voluntary Service

Box, J. (2001) 'Advocacy and empowerment: an evaluation of Knowsley Pensioners Advocacy and Information Service', MA dissertation, University of Liverpool

Brandon, D. (1998) 'Mental health advocacy', in Y. Craig (ed.) *Advocacy, Counselling and Meditation Casework.* London: Jessica Kingsley

Brandon, D. with Brandon, A. and Brandon, T. (1995) *Advocacy – Power to People With Disabilities.* Birmingham: Venture Press

British Medical Association (1995) *The Older Person: Consent and Care*, Report of the British Medical Association and the Royal College of Nursing. London: British Medical Association

Cambridgeshire County Council Social Services (2002) *Advocacy Handbook.* www.camcnty.gov.uk/sub/ssd/advocacy/index.htm

Card, H. (1990) 'Senior citizen advocacy', *Open Mind*, No. 45 (June/July), p. 17

Cawthra, L. (1999) 'Older people's health information needs', *Health Libraries Review*, Vol. 16, pp. 97–105

Cohen, P. (1994) 'Advocates of independence', *Nursing Times*, Vol. 90, No. 9, pp. 66–9

Cohen, P. (1995) 'Speaking up for others', *Nursing Times*, Vol. 91, No. 13, pp. 54–5

Department of Health (2001) *National Service Framework for Older People*. London: Department of Health

Department of Health (2002) *Supporting the Implementation of Patient Advice and Liaison Services. A Resource Pack*. London: Department of Health

Dunning, A. (1995) *Citizen Advocacy With Older People: A Code of Good Practice*. London: Centre for Policy on Ageing

Dunning, A. (1998a) 'Information is power', *Open Mind*, Vol. 90 (March/April), p. 11

Dunning, A. (1998b) 'House of representatives', *Community Care*, 16–22 April, p. 15

Dunning, A. (1999) 'Policy, programmes and perspectives', *Generations Review*, Vol. 9, No. 1, p. 20

Ellis, T. (1999) 'Improving access to information for older people', *Innovations in Information*, Vol. 5, No. 3, pp. 6–7

EPPI-Centre (2002) *Core Keywording Strategy*, Data collection for a register of educational research. London: EPPI-Centre, Social Science Research Unit

George, M. (1991) 'Do it yourself', *Community Care*, 9 May, pp. 21–3

Goldsmith, M. (1996) *Hearing the Voice of People with Dementia*. London: Jessica Kingsley

Hayden, C. and Boaz, A. (2000) *Making a Difference: Better Government for Older People Evaluation Report*. www.bgop.org.uk/reference/pub178.htm

Hayden, C., Boaz, A. and Taylor, F. (2001) *Attitudes and Aspirations of Older People: A Qualitative Study*. www.dss.gov.uk/asd/asd5/102summ.html

Help the Aged (2001) *Annual Report and Accounts*. London: Age Concern

Hinkley, P. and Steele, J. (1992) *National Disability Information Provision: Sources and Issues*. London: Policy Studies Institute

Ivers, V. (1994) *Citizen Advocacy in Action: Working with Older People*. Stoke-on-Trent: Beth Johnson Foundation Publications

Kelly, N. (2000) *Mind Guide to Advocacy*. London: Mind

Lawson, J. (2002) Personal communication. Post Doctoral Fellow, Institute of Health and Social Care Research, University of Salford.

Lindsay, M. (1997) 'Balancing Power: Advocacy in a Scottish Health Board Area'. *Research, Policy and Planning*, Vol. 15, No. 2, pp. 31–3

McManus, O. (1999) 'A centre for the voice of dementia', *Working With Older People*, July, pp. 23–7

May, H. (1998) 'Information for older people: a vital but missing link in community care', *Managing Community Care*, Vol. 6, No. 2, pp. 76–84

Morgan, G. (undated) *Proposals for Development of Advocacy in Highland*, cited in D. Atkinson (1999) *Advocacy: A Review*. Brighton: Pavilion Publishing/Joseph Rowntree Foundation

Older People's Advocacy Alliance (OPAAL) (2000) Help the Aged news release, 25 July

O'Neill Crossman, R. (1994) 'Empowerment and community care for the elderly', *Voluntary Voice*, October, p. 9

Research Update (2002) *Prevention Works*. Kidlington: Anchor Trust

Scottish Executive (2001) *Independent Advocacy: A Guide for Commissioners*. www.scotland.gov.uk/library3/health/iagc-01.asp (accessed 22 July 2002)

Searle, P. (2001) 'Care Direct – what is it and how is it being developed?', *Managing Community Care*, Vol. 9, No. 5, pp. 37–41

Simons, K. (1993) *Citizen Advocacy: The Inside View*. Bristol: The Norah Fry Research Centre, University of Bristol

Tester, S. (1992) *Common Knowledge: A Coordinated Approach to Information-Giving*. London: Centre for Policy on Ageing

Tester, S. and Meredith, B. (1987) *Ill Informed? A Study of Information and Support for Elderly People in the Inner City*. London: Policy Studies Institute

Thornton, P. and Tozer, R. (1994) *Involving Older People in Planning and Evaluating Community Care: A Review of Initiatives*. York: Social Policy Research Unit, University of York

Valios, N. (2001) 'Welfare hotline', *Community Care*, 15–21 November, pp. 30–1

Valios, N. (2002) 'Spoken for', *Community Care*, 18–24 April, pp. 32–3

Wertheimer, A. (1993) *Speaking Out: Citizen Advocacy and Older People* London: Centre for Policy on Ageing,

Williams, S. (1999) 'Advocacy and communication', in V. Tschudin (ed.) *Counselling and Older People: An Introductory Guide*. London: Age Concern

Appendix

Examples of advocacy projects

- Trafford CVS Advocacy Scheme

- The Alan McLure House Advocacy Project (1999)

- The Fife Advocacy Project

- The North Staffordshire Advocacy and Older People Project

- The Alzheimers Disease Society Advocacy Scheme, Berkshire

- The Isle of Wight Advocacy Consortium

- Age Concern Coventry's Advocacy Service

- Advocacy Partners, Surrey

- The Standing Conference of Ethnic Minority Senior Citizens

- Age Concern Advocacy Project Walsall

- Westminster Advocacy Service for Senior Residents

- African-Caribbean Resource Centre in Nottingham

- Help the Aged Dignity on the Ward Campaign

- Age Concern Tendring Advocacy Scheme

- North Manchester Pensioners Association's LINKAGE Project

- Knowsley Pensioners Advocacy and Information Service

Organisations which support and promote advocacy projects

- Mind

- Age Concern England

- Citizen Advocacy, Information and Training (CAIT)

- Advocacy Across London

- Advocacy Council, Surrey

- The Highland Community Care Forum

- Sense Advocacy Development Network

- The Older People's Advocacy Alliance (OPAAL)

- North Manchester Pensioners Association

- Cambridgeshire County Council Social Services Department

- Enfield Council for Voluntary Service

- Alzheimer's Society

- Greater London Forum for the Elderly